ROYAL
CORONATIONS

Lucinda Gosling

SHIRE PUBLICATIONS

Published in Great Britain in 2013 by Shire Publications Ltd, Midland House, West Way, Botley, Oxford OX2 0PH, United Kingdom.

43-01 21st Street, Suite 220B, Long Island City, NY 11101, USA.

E-mail: shire@shirebooks.co.uk   www.shirebooks.co.uk

A CIP catalogue record for this book is available from the British Library.

Shire Library no. 726.   ISBN-13: 978 0 74781 220 3

Lucinda Gosling has asserted her right under the Copyright, Designs and Patents Act, 1988, to be identified as the author of this book.

Designed by Tony Truscott Designs, Sussex, UK and typeset in Perpetua and Gill Sans.

Printed in China through Worldprint Ltd.

13 14 15 16 17   10 9 8 7 6 5 4 3 2 1

COVER IMAGE
Queen Elizabeth II, pictured on the front cover of John Bull magazine in June 1953, flanked by clergy and followed by her train-bearing Maids of Honour. After several costume changes during the course of the ceremony, her robe of ermine and purple velvet, the Imperial State Crown and the Sceptre and Orb form the final and iconic image of her as monarch as she leaves Westminster Abbey.

TITLE PAGE IMAGE
The coronation procession of George V passes along the Mall, through Admiralty Arch and into Trafalgar Square on its way to Westminster Abbey on 22 June 1911.

CONTENTS PAGE IMAGE
An allegorical illustration by Byam Shaw (1872–1919), published in The Sphere on 24 June 1911 as part of its coverage of the coronation, showing past monarchs of Britain hailing the newly crowned and enthroned King George V and Queen Mary.

ACKNOWLEDGEMENTS
My thanks to Peter Urbach at the Reform Club for showing me the club's fascinating archive of Coronation material, Kate Wigley at the Warner Textile Archive for her information on the company's royal connections and to Mary Evans Picture Library for their help with images. In addition, I'm grateful to Ruth Sheppard for her inexhaustible supply of patience, encouragement and sound advice.

PHOTOGRAPH ACKNOWLEDGEMENTS
Grenville Collins Postcard Collection/Mary Evans Picture Library, page 49 (top); Hardy Amies/Mary Evans Picture Library, page 20; Iberfoto/Mary Evans Picture Library, page 6; Illustrated London News Archive/Mary Evans Picture Library, pages 3, 8, 9, 10, 11, 12, 16, 17, 18 (top), 21, 22 (both), 23, 24, 26, 27 (top), 28, 29, 30 (bottom), 32, 36 (bottom), 37, 38, 39, 40, 41, 42, 43, 44, 45, 48 (top), 49 (bottom), 50, 51, 53, 56, 58 (bottom), 60 (top), 61; Interfoto/Mary Evans Picture Library, 4; Mary Evans Picture Library, 7, 15 (top), 18 (bottom), 19, 27 (bottom), 34 (both), 46, 48 (bottom), 58 (top); TP Archive/Mary Evans Picture Library, 14 (right). All other images are from the author's collection.

Shire Publications is supporting the Woodland Trust, the UK's leading woodland conservation charity, by funding the dedication of trees.

CONTENTS

Apres son regna henry le tex sun fiz. lui. aunz
fuit de .ix. aunz de age quant fuit corone. e en
cene fuit la bataylle de Euesham. ou fuit occys
Symund de munfort. e sun fiz henry. e syre hugh
penser e muz des barons e des chevalers de co-
tre. puis moust cyl henry le roy. e gist a Westm

ORIGINS AND HISTORY

ON 2 June 1953, millions sat in living rooms across the United Kingdom to watch one of the most celebrated events of the twentieth century. For over three hours, families, friends and neighbours huddled around the small screens of recently purchased television sets. Through a grey, miasmic fog they could just about make out the young queen solemnly giving a faultless performance as she went through the rituals of a centuries-old ceremony. It cannot have escaped the notice of many that they were in the privileged position of witnessing the coronation – an inauguration ceremony with the most remarkable longevity dating back more than one thousand years – through one of the most recent inventions of the modern age.

The first account of an English coronation comes in a life of St Oswald, Archbishop of York, written by the monk of Ramsay in around the year 1000. King Edgar's coronation, presided over by St Dunstan, Archbishop of Canterbury, took place at Bath, on Pentecost, the feast of the Holy Spirit, in 973; the features of the 1953 coronation bear striking similarities to those recorded at the beginning of the eleventh century. Edgar, the great-grandson of King Alfred of Wessex, was anointed, invested with an orb and sceptre and acclaimed with the familiar cries of, 'Long Live the King, may the king live forever.' The anthem *Zadok the Priest and Nathan the Prophet* was sung and later, at Chester, six other kings of Britain came to swear their allegiance. Taking place fourteen years after he came to the throne, Edgar's coronation was a ceremony intended to celebrate the glorious culmination of his reign, not an initiation rite. Nevertheless, all the elements of his coronation are otherwise found in its modern-day counterpart.

These features had been found variously but not wholly in recognising previous kings. The defining ritual of royal unction, the anointing with fragrant holy oil (chrism), representing the Holy Spirit, dated back to the Old Testament. There were references to the practice in Celtic Ireland and Visigothic Spain from the end of the seventh century, and a life of St Columba recounts the story of the saint anointing Aidan, king of Dalraida, as far back as 571. The Frankish king, Pepin I, was anointed first at Soissons in 752 and a

Opposite:
Henry III (1207–72) rebuilt Westminster Abbey during his reign, drafting in French architects to remodel it in a Gothic style based on the cathedral of Reims. At great expense, Henry created a fitting ceremonial space for future coronations and a shrine to the Abbey's original founder, Edward the Confessor. Henry himself underwent two coronations: the first at the age of nine in Gloucester, when he acceded the throne, and the second in 1220 at Westminster Abbey when he reached adulthood.

The coronation of Charlemagne, King of the Franks and Holy Roman Emperor, on Christmas Day, 800, as depicted in an illuminated fourteenth-century manuscript. It shows Pope Leo X placing a crown on Charlemagne's head – a novel concept in the ninth century but one that was to form the central focus of the coronation ceremony in the following centuries.

second time in 754 at the Basilica of St Denis by Pope Stephen II, but the coronation of Pepin's son, Charlemagne, as Holy Roman Emperor by Pope Leo III in Rome on Christmas Day 800 set a blueprint for other kings of Western Europe: Charlemagne was crowned.

It was these two biblically inspired actions, the anointing and the crowning, which formed the basis for the coronation service; glued together with more pagan features such as the carrying of spears or long staffs, and the use of a throne, an idea first imported by the Vikings. The Christianisation of Europe during these years meant that, in the days before primogeniture, kings could have their claims supported and their actions sanctioned through consecration during a powerfully symbolic and spiritual ceremony. In an age when church and state became integrally bound, it gave a king mystique, portrayed him as pious as well as powerful and, above all, gave him the spiritual stamp of approval.

What we know about the coronation service from the medieval era is documented in surviving liturgical texts known as *ordines*, or *recensions*. Of the four major documents tracing the development of the English coronation, two pre-date the Norman Conquest and while they tell us what blessings and prayers were said, and their sequence, there are no rubrics (ecclesiastical stage directions). We know what was said, but we do not know how this was arranged, what was worn or what might have been sung. The First Recension, is represented in three separate texts including the Leofric Missal, which dates from around 900, was written at the Abbey of St Vaast and brought to England by Leofric, Bishop of Exeter. It marks out the coronation ceremony in the clearly defined stages we might recognise today – election, oath, consecration, unction, investiture and blessing. Scholarly debate continues as to whether this first *ordo* was ever used for any actual ceremonies in England. The Second Recension, of which at least five text versions survive, introduces new items of regalia such as the ring and the sword. It also records the role of the queen consort and her anointing as an important and integral part of the ceremony. It is this version of the coronation script that was followed by King Edgar in 973, though information about other coronations beyond that is frustratingly scant.

The Bayeux Tapestry brings us some visual idea of kingship by the eleventh century. King Harold, whose brief and quickly contested reign followed the death of Edward the Confessor in 1066, sits on what looks very much like a throne. On his head is a crown with *fleuron* (lily-shaped pinnacles) and around his shoulders, a royal mantle. He holds in one hand a *baculus* (rod) and in the other, an orb. His appearance, adorned with the familiar symbols of sovereignty, is one we recognise today. There is no written evidence to confirm it, but as Harold was at Westminster when Edward died and was crowned hurriedly the following day, the assumption is that he was crowned at Westminster Abbey. What is certain is that his usurper William, Duke of Normandy, was crowned there, on Christmas Day 1066, establishing the abbey as the setting for all future English coronations, of which there have been thirty-eight in total.

The abbey has always had close links with royalty. King Edgar was the first benefactor, giving the monastic community at Westminster substantial lands. A century later, King Edward (later Edward the Confessor, whose own coronation took place at Winchester) established his palace close by and built a large stone church that was to become his own burial place.

A detail from the Bayeux Tapestry depicting King Harold at the beginning of his short-lived reign in 1066, clearly seated on an elevated throne and holding a sceptre-like rod and orb, all recognised elements of the modern-day coronation.

The abbey was a shrewd choice of venue for William I's coronation, linking him with Edward the Confessor to legitimise his claim and decisively cancelling out that of the defeated Harold. A century on from Edgar's, the coronation's format was edging ever closer to that of the modern coronation, beginning with a great procession involving not only monks and clergy, but also the great magnates of the realm. Another innovation was that during the ceremony the king sat on a dais, thus raising him up above his subjects, symbolically as well as physically.

The coronation of Richard I in 1189 appears to have been a lavish affair. Roger of Wendover's account included a description of the procession with nobles carrying the sceptres, spurs, and swords and a golden canopy over the king's head.

At the coronation of Richard I in 1189, the first to be reported in detail (by Roger of Wendover), yet more familiar features become apparent. The account describes how the king was supported by the bishops of Durham and Bath and Wells, and how the procession included nobles carrying the regalia.

Then came Godfrey de Lucy carrying the king's coif (cap), and John Marshal by him carrying two great and weighty golden spurs. Next came William Marshal, Earl of Strigul, carrying the royal sceptre on the top of which was a golden cross, and William de Patryrick, Earl of Salisbury, by his side, bearing a golden rod with a golden dove on top.

Roger also listed three dukes bearing royal swords with golden scabbards, and a golden canopy was held over Richard's head by four barons.

Henry III's re-building of the Confessor's church in the mid-thirteenth century acknowledged the need for a dedicated space, known as the 'theatre', to accommodate the persons and rituals necessary in a coronation. Consequently, its plan follows that of Reims Cathedral, the coronation church of French kings, with a square area between the choir and the sanctuary large enough for the ceremony to take place. In recent coronations, this area has been carpeted in a yellow gold colour, providing a glowing stage.

The lengthy interval between accession and coronation in recent centuries, required to organise the event but also partly out of respect for the late monarch, found no counterpart in the Middle Ages when coronations took place with what we might view as unseemly haste. An exception was Edward I, who was in the Holy Land fighting the Crusades when he became king in 1272. After a leisurely return to England, his coronation took place in the new abbey on 19 August 1274 with his beloved queen, Eleanor of Castile, crowned beside him. The coronation banquet held at Westminster Hall afterwards – a custom that lasted from the thirteenth century to the reign of William IV in 1831 – saw no expense spared, with 430 sheep, 380 heads of cattle, eighteen wild boars and nearly 20,000 capons and fowls requisitioned for the feast.

Through the medieval period, the coronation ceremony continued to be adapted and re-written. The Third Recension, known as the Order of Henry I, dates from the twelfth century and is found in a Canterbury Pontifical, while the Fourth dates from the fourteenth century; a version of it seems to have first been used at the coronation of Edward II. The *ordines* are recorded in two beautifully illuminated books, the *Litlyngton Missal* and

A magnificent cutaway illustration of Westminster Abbey by Douglas Macpherson in *The Sphere*'s record of the 1937 coronation of George VI, revealing its interior with the additional seating and the yellow-carpeted theatre where the ceremony would take place.

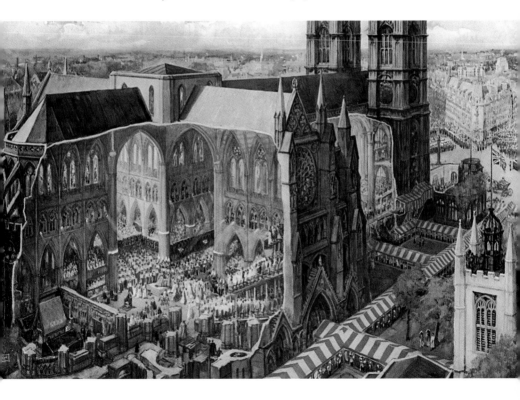

The crowning of a queen from the *Liber Regalis*, a manuscript outlining the order of coronation services from the fourteenth century. It was probably created for Richard II's queen, Anne of Bohemia, whose crowning took place a few days after her marriage in 1382.

Opposite: The Abbey's theatre with its golden-yellow carpet, showing the moment after Queen Elizabeth II was crowned and received the blessing from the Archbishop of Canterbury. The Great Officers and bearers of the regalia have taken up their places behind the crimson throne, and the archbishop, the dean and the bishops' assistants move from the Chair to the Throne in readiness for the Enthronisation. On either side of the queen stand the bishops of Durham and Bath and Wells in readiness to conduct her to the Throne, and before her stands the Marquess of Salisbury, who will precede her with the jewelled Sword of State.

the celebrated *Liber Regalis*, bothpreserved in Westminster Abbey's library. These documents provided the order of service for all subsequent coronations up to and including that of Elizabeth I, with occasional amendments to suit the political or religious circumstances. The service was shortened somewhat for the coronation of Edward VI, partly on account of his age, and in 1601 the liturgy was translated from Latin to English for the coronation of James I. Monarchs have always been crowned in the context of the Eucharist or Holy Communion but in 1685, William Sancroft, Archbishop of Canterbury, was assigned the task of eliminating the communion service for the Catholic James II, much to the disapproval of many including diarist John Evelyn, who wrote, '(to the greate sorrow of the people) no Sacrament, as ought to have ben.' James II's coronation was also, incidentally, the first time a monarch was invested with the orb. Just four years later, much of the axed coronation service was restored with amendments instead to reflect the joint coronation of James's daughter Mary and her husband, William of Orange.

The coronation of Edward VII in 1902, coming more than sixty years after that of his mother, Queen Victoria, saw some re-shaping of the service in the capable hands of Lord Esher, secretary of the Office of Works, whose knowledge of the ceremonial minutiae proved invaluable. At Esher's suggestion, several ancient customs were revived but within a modern context. The Dymoke family had for centuries acted the role of King's Champion, appearing at the coronation banquet on horseback to challenge any of the sovereign's detractors. The banquet, and therefore the champion, was now dispensed with, but in 1953, Captain J. L. Marmion Dymoke, a descendant of the last King's Champion, still attended the queen but in the full dress uniform of the 1st Battalion of the Royal Lincolnshire Regiment rather than a suit of armour, and bearing one of the royal standards. The barons of the Cinque Ports, traditionally the bearers of the canopy, were allowed to walk in the procession and act as recipients for the banners in the Abbey. It was an attempt to restore the traditional chivalric elements of the medieval ceremony, but to carry it out with twentieth-century efficiency, an aim that found its full expression with the coronation of Elizabeth II.

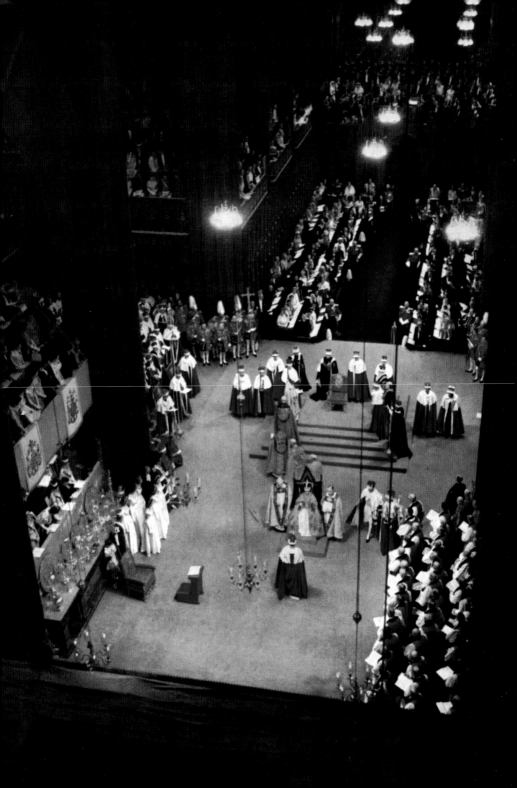

PLANNING A
CORONATION

O N 7 June 1952, the coronation proclamation was read out at four sites
in London, traditionally visited on such occasions. At St James's Palace,
Charing Cross, Temple Bar and finally, the Royal Exchange in the City of
London, the proclamation declared, 'Her Majesty's Pleasure touching her
Royal Coronation and the Solemnity thereof', stating the intended date of
the coronation as 2 June the following year.

This quaint heraldic ceremony publicly launched the coronation's
preparations in 1952, though a Coronation Commission had already been
formed in May and was busily working behind the scenes with Prince Philip,
Duke of Edinburgh, as chairman and other members including Winston
Churchill, Lord Woolton and Geoffrey Francis Fisher, Archbishop of
Canterbury. The lynchpin of this group was the Earl Marshal, a title held
since the reign of Charles II by the Howard family, the hereditary dukes
of Norfolk. The Earl Marshal's responsibility, as head of an Executive
Coronation Commission, was as organiser-in-chief, overseeing the practical
considerations of just about every ceremonial aspect of the coronation from
the processional route to the programme of celebratory events. Bernard
Marmaduke Fitzalan Howard, sixteenth Duke of Norfolk, who inherited
the dukedom at the age of nine, had served in the Sussex Regiment and had
brought to the coronation of George VI the brisk efficiency bestowed by
a military career. On that occasion he had greeted the eleven-year-old
heir-presumptive, Princess Elizabeth, on her arrival at the Abbey, and
sixteen years later he reprised his role for her coronation.

The Earl Marshal was also the traditional head of the College of Arms,
comprising of four kings-at-arms, six heralds and four pursuivants. This
ancient institution, granted a charter by Richard III in 1484, was part of
the royal household, though self-funded. It not only kept records of coats
of arms, but, as a development of the heralds' original role organising royal
tournaments, supported the Earl Marshal in the oldest royal ceremonials
and rituals, recording and archiving what had gone before at previous
coronations and marshalling the procession to ensure that participants walked

Opposite:
Piccadilly Circus
in London,
adorned with flags
and specially
designed street
decorations in
honour of the
coronation of
George VI in
May 1937.
Painting by
Henry C. Brewer,
reproduced in
The Illustrated
London News.

Right: The Garter Principal King-at-Arms from the College of Arms, proclaims the date of the coronation of Queen Elizabeth II as 2 June 1953 at Stable Yard, St James's Palace. Standing to his left is the Right Honourable Bernard Marmaduke Howard, sixteenth Duke of Norfolk and Earl Marshal, who was responsible for organising all practical aspects of the coronation.

Far right: Front cover of *Men Only* magazine, with the Earl Marshal caricatured by Edward Hynes. The duke was responsible for ceremonial arrangements on behalf of the monarchy, and organised the coronations of both George VI in 1937 and Elizabeth II in 1953.

in order according to their status. In essence, the heralds ensured everything was done properly and with a precise respect for the past. Their participation in the coronation procession allowed for a peacock display of medieval finery as they donned their colourful tabards embroidered with the royal arms.

The Court of Claims, announced at the same time as the planned date of the coronation, was perhaps the most unusual curiosity associated with the coronation. The first Court of Claims was held by John of Gaunt, uncle of King Richard II, and sat in the White Hall of Westminster Palace. It listened to the claims of those who either through family tradition or status wished to render the sovereign some personal service during the coronation. Many of the potential 'jobs' seem spectacularly unnecessary, such as that of the Lord of the Manor of Farnham Royal, who claimed to support the king's right arm while he held the sceptre. There was also the Chief Lardiner, who managed the larder for the coronation banquet and whose payment was in any leftovers. Contemporary illustrations of the coronation procession from the late Stuart and Georgian periods show another long-since obsolete role, that of a herb-strewer or herbswoman, last seen at the coronation of George IV, when it was performed by Anne Fellowes who cast rosebuds in the path of the king.

Besides the Earl Marshal, other lay roles of importance include the Lord Great Chamberlain, whose domain is Westminster Hall where the coronation procession used to assemble before setting out for the abbey, and where the coronation banquet would take place afterwards (the last one during the reign of George IV). In earlier coronations the Lord Great Chamberlain would also watch over the sovereign the night before the coronation and bring him his shirt and robes in the morning, for which responsibility he received the remuneration of forty yards of velvet and the king's bed! By the twentieth century, the role of Lord Great Chamberlain was distilled down to a formal one – offering the spurs to the monarch during the ceremony – though he also is in attendance at the state opening of Parliament and at state funerals.

Two other offices, revived solely for each coronation, are those of the Lord High Steward, who walks before the monarch in the procession, carrying St Edward's Crown, and the Lord High Constable, who attends the sovereign bearing his staff of office in his hand and assists in the delivery of the regalia to the dean and chapter of Westminster.

The Archbishop of Canterbury has had the privilege of conferring the crown since the time of William I, and has presided at all coronations at Westminster Abbey except for that of Henry I, Edward II, Mary I, and William and Mary. In the case of the latter, William Sancroft, Archbishop of Canterbury, had remained loyal to the ousted James II and it was Henry Compton, Bishop of London, who crowned the king and queen. In other cases, expediency played a part. Henry I was crowned within just three days of the death of William II and the exiled Archbishop Anselm was simply unavailable at such short notice. The Archbishop of Canterbury is supported during the ceremony by the Archbishop of York, whose duties extend to crowning the queen consort and acting as her chaplain. The Bishop of Durham walks on the sovereign's right-hand side and the Bishop of Bath and Wells walks on the left, while the Dean of Westminster instructs the monarch in the rites and ceremonies of the coronation and assists the Archbishop of Canterbury throughout.

With the main roles and supporting players confirmed, the preparations for a coronation can gather pace. The time between accession and coronation, typically at least a year since the beginning of the nineteenth century, not only allows for the practical arrangements to be carried out, but is also important in giving

One of the ancient roles played out during the coronation was that of the King's Herbswoman, who, along with six maiden helpers, strewed petals along the king's path into Westminster Abbey.

Front cover of *The Sphere* from 1 May 1937 depicting a splendidly attired herald on horseback blowing his ceremonial trumpet in honour of the coronation of King George VI on 12 May 1937.

A view inside the Great Hall, a temporary annexe designed by Sir James West and built onto Westminster Abbey for the coronation of King George VI in 1937. The modern building's interior was hung with tapestries; under one, the regalia are set out ready to be carried into the abbey ahead of the procession.

overseas guests sufficient notice. At the 1902 coronation of Edward VII, three hundred seats were reserved for premiers and governors from various parts of the empire, including the numerous maharajahs and other Indian dignitaries. Seating had to be found for other sections of the congregation — 568 for the Foreign Office, 350 for the Admiralty, 400 for the War Office, 183 for the India Office and 235 for the Civil Service. Added to that were the hundreds of peers and peeresses, members of Parliament, courtiers, the mayors of London boroughs, councillors, and representatives of other faiths, medical, legal and learned societies as well as high-ranking officers of the Armed Forces. The abbey, with a capacity of two thousand, had to be adapted to accommodate a congregation of 6,603. By the coronation of George V the number had risen to 7,139 and for the coronation of Elizabeth II, capacity had to be quadrupled to 8,200.

The solution was to build and extend upwards, a large-scale building project instructed by the Earl Marshal and carried out by the Office of Works. It required the abbey to close for months while scaffolding was erected to provide tiered galleries and seating in every conceivable nook, cranny and eyrie giving what for many must have been a frustratingly fleeting glimpse of the events far below. The problem was a perennial one. For the coronation of Charles II in 1661, Sir Edward Walker, given the task of organising it, wrote of the scaffolds in the north transept, 'for persons of all Conditions to sitt and behold this great & Sacred Solemnity'. The diarist Samuel Pepys sat here, but complained about the view and was obliged to leave before the end as he 'had so great a liste to piss.' For the coronation of Queen Anne, the Earl Marshal instructed Sir Christopher Wren to 'make Galleries and Seats for as many as possible on each side of the Quire & Great Theatre'. Such alterations inevitably took their toll on the medieval masonry of the abbey, and the writer Robert Huish, recorded how workmen in the abbey prior to the coronation of George III would boast that they had 'broken the noses, and cut off the ears of a whole legion of angels.' Thankfully, by 1821, there was a more enlightened, conservative approach and the monuments were boarded over for protection. Notices around the abbey in 1953 reminded workers, 'Remember the building in which you work is sacred. You are earnestly asked to be reverent in your demeanour and careful of the fabric and monuments.'

Since the coronation of William IV in 1831, the abbey's alterations have included the addition of an annexe on to the West Front, a large space where the coronation procession could assemble before moving into the abbey itself. Although temporary, these were significant structures, designed at first to blend seamlessly with the Gothic style of the abbey. Then, in 1937, a design by Sir James West offered a striking modernist counterpoint to the ancient building. The annexe for Elizabeth II's coronation was pure mid-century, looking as if it could have been lifted straight from the Festival of Britain site.

But such modern design interventions were an exception. Even the interior of the 1937 annexe was hung with tapestries borrowed from the dukes of

An illustration by Dennis Flanders in *The Sphere*, showing the modern mid-century annexe temporarily built to accommodate the 1953 coronation procession as it entered and departed the abbey. Designed by Eric Bedford at a cost of £50,000, the annexe took almost six months to build and also contained special rooms for robing and retiring. Its exterior was guarded by a line of heraldic statues of the 'Queen's Beasts'.

The thrones used for the enthronement stage of the ceremony during the coronation of George V in June 1911 were reproduced by Messrs Morris (William Morris) from Jacobean originals at Knole.

At the time of his coronation, George IV was fifty-eight years old and obese, but his vanity still led him to choose an extravagant costume.

Buccleuch. Tradition ran through almost every aspect of coronation preparations. Warner & Sons in Braintree, Essex, had woven the rich fabrics for the coronation since the reign of Queen Victoria. In 1953, they set a Mr Spinks, who had first started at the company in 1910 at the age of seventeen, to work on the trial piece of a design called Queensway to ensure that the correct combination of gold thread and blue silk was used. Two other old hands, Lily Lee and Hilda Carver, came out of retirement to hand-weave the silk velvet; a job for which only they had the expertise. In the end, almost one mile of the Queensway fabric was woven (using lurex thread instead of the gold used in previous coronations due to post-war privations) and when Warner & Sons opened its doors to the public over one weekend, queues stretched down the street from the early hours as people waited patiently to see the unique fabric being woven before their eyes. For the 1911 coronation of George V, the coronation thrones were upholstered with crimson silk damask specially designed by the artist and craftsman William Morris some years before. The silk was dyed with pure madder and woven on the Morris handlooms at Merton Abbey. The coronation was, after all, the ultimate opportunity to showcase the very best of British industry and craftsmanship.

Tradition and symbolism were essential for the clothes worn by the participants too. Beyond the ceremonial vestments, a symbolic part of the coronation ceremony, the choice of coronation dress allowed the monarch or consort to display a mix of personal taste, ancient tradition, patriotic credentials and splendour. Few coronation costumes have been more idiosyncratic or representative of their wearer's taste than that of George IV: a cloth-of-silver doublet and trunk hose, lavishly trimmed with gold lace and braid. The fabric for Queen Mary's coronation dress was woven by Warner's and designed by court dressmakers Reville and Rossiter. The embroidered pattern of English rose, Scottish thistle, Irish shamrock, star of India, lotus of India and English oak leaves and acorns were all worked in the finest gold thread by ladies of the Princess Louise Needlework School in Sloane Street while the silk velvet robe and train was woven in Sudbury, a centre for silk weaving since the eighteenth century. This emphasis on

By the beginning of the twentieth century, subjects around the Empire contributed to the coronation of Edward VII. The superb overdress of Indian embroidery made for Queen Alexandra was worked in Delhi during the winter of 1901–2 by forty of the most skilled needleworkers at the firm of Manick Chand (the white-robed figure leaning over the table). The man crouched on the floor to the left is Ashraf Khan, who designed the piece.

supporting British industries extended to the empire too and in 1901, the fabric for Queen Alexandra's coronation dress was worked by skilled needleworkers in India.

Nobody was surprised when Sir Norman Hartnell, already an established couturier to royalty and designer of the queen's wedding dress in 1947, was tasked with designing the gown for the 1953 coronation, but nevertheless, speculation over its design was at fever pitch. Out of the nine separate designs submitted by Hartnell, the one chosen was an elaborately embroidered work of art, incorporating the floral emblems of England, Ireland, Scotland, Wales and the Dominions in an allegorical feast of silk thread, seed pearls and crystals. Security was of the utmost importance. Press tried to rent space in the mews opposite Hartnell's workrooms and use long-focus cameras, so at first the girls working on the dress were not told the significance of their project. They were placed in a room by themselves and the dress was covered in tissue to avoid any spying. The precautions were worthwhile and the queen declared the gown 'Glorious!' when it was finally unveiled.

Hartnell had his work cut out for him. Not only had he designed the dress for the leading lady but for the supporting cast too; the Queen Mother, Princess Margaret, and the six maids-of-honour were all dressed by Hartnell; even the new robe design for peeresses, not updated since the reign of Queen Anne, was down to him.

It was not only the human participants who had to look their best for the coronation. The horses destined for the procession, and in particular the famous creams (later replaced with greys) who would pull the magnificent state coach, were prepared for their big day at the Royal Mews, under the supervision of Lord Beaufort, Master of the Horse. Their full state harness, with its great gilt studs and medallions bearing the royal arms, was polished until it gleamed and they were put through their paces with a trial run along the processional route. On the day of the 1911 coronation rehearsal, members of the public were recruited to wave flags, cheer and bang drums, ensuring that on the day itself, the horses would be unfazed by the cacophony of sound.

Others taking part in the event assembled in London in the weeks leading up to the coronation, and accommodation had to be found for the hundreds of colonial troops who would march in the procession. Some were billeted near Sloane Square in the grounds of the old Duke of York's Military School, others in Hyde Park,

Opposite: The design for the magnificent coronation dress of Queen Elizabeth II created by couturier Norman Hartnell. The gown featured exquisitely intricate embroidery, a hallmark of Hartnell's work, depicting the various floral symbols of the British Isles and Commonwealth countries.

George Grey Wornum (1888–1957), British architect, pictured at his drawing board designing street decorations for the coronation of King George VI in 1937.

Health and safety checks – policemen test the strength of the viewing stands along the processional route for the coronation of King George V. Viewing platforms, galleries and stands were erected all around Westminster and its environs.

An obedient Chow dog waits patiently while its owner watches the coronation rehearsal prior to the real event on 12 May 1937. With tickets for viewing the coronation at a premium, even rehearsals found enthusiastic spectators.

which became a sea of tents, but the Indian contingent for the coronations of both George V and Edward VII were stationed in the splendid surroundings of Hampton Court Palace, where crowds gathered daily to watch the Sikhs indulge in their favourite pastime, the game of quoits.

The building of stands and galleries along the processional route, to provide as much opportunity as possible for the public to see their newly crowned monarch turned London temporarily into a building site. *The Sphere* in 1911 ran a double-page spread of photographs illustrating 'How the Metropolis Disappeared Under a Maze of Timber' and estimated that £150,000 had been spent on wood and labour for the temporary structures. Street decorations too needed months of planning and preparation. Sir High Casson, the architect and artist in charge of adorning London for the 1953 coronation, placed them centrally along the processional routes so that they would not be obscured by nearby buildings. Sir Grey Wornum, who was responsible for the decorations along most of the 1937 route, listed the practical challenges he faced in an interview published in *The Sphere*.

'We have had to consider traffic, the objections of people who were afraid their view would be spoiled, the necessity of sticking to what you can do instead of going after what you'd like to do, and, last but not least, the delicate matter of digging fresh holes for pole sockets in London streets.'

Viewing points and rehearsals took on a more significant complexion in 1953 when the BBC faced the challenge of its biggest outside broadcast in the history of the service. Film cameras had been present at the coronation of George VI, cunningly concealed behind the tomb of Aymer de Valence. But a live transmission was an ambitious step forward, requiring a planning committee at the corporation to work on timetables and logistics during the twelve months preceding the event. Six cameras were located in the abbey itself as well as a large number of microphones, which had to be inconspicuous. Camera operators of slight build were selected, such was the limitation on space, especially above the organ. Fifteen more cameras were positioned along the processional route together with commentators and for televison viewers at home, the ceremony was accompanied by the poetic commentary of Richard Dimbleby. Despite initial apprehension from some quarters as to the wisdom of televising the ceremony (some thought that it put unnecessary pressure on the queen, others felt it compromised the solemnity of the occasion) the landmark broadcast was considered a success, owing in no small part to the breathtakingly accurate timing on the day. On 3 March 1953, the Earl Marshal had announced to the world that the queen would be crowned at 'about 12.34' and so she was, give or take a few seconds. Such punctuality was a gift to the BBC. For them, and for the millions who watched the coronation on televisions and in cinemas around the globe, the planning had all been worthwhile.

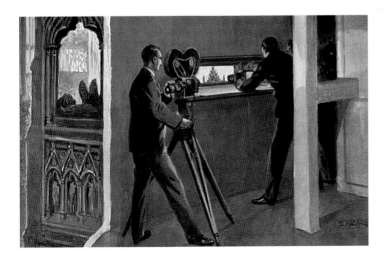

Cinematographers filmed the coronation of George VI in 1937 from a discreet position constructed behind the tomb of Aymer de Valence in the abbey sanctuary, looking through a small window to the coronation theatre. Completely hidden from view, the chamber was also soundproofed with plate glass in the slot window and padding on the wall.

REGALIA

EVERY YEAR, the Tower of London, London's top visitor attraction, welcomes almost two and a half million visitors. The majority will stand on the moving walkways that take them on a frustratingly rapid tour past the glitter and glint of the world-famous crown jewels in the Jewel House. The tower has been the custodian of the crown jewels since 1661, when the jewels were newly created. The execution of Charles I in 1649 and the abolition of the monarchy led to an order from the Lord Protector, Oliver Cromwell, that the crowns and other regalia symbolic of monarchy be forcibly seized and destroyed, so men acting for Parliament 'broake into the Jewel House and took away ... three crowns, two sceptres, [and] bracelets'. The gold and silver was sent to the Royal Mint, also at the tower, to be melted down and made into coins; the gemstones were first removed from their settings and then sold. The only items to survive were the three steel swords of state and the twelfth-century gold anointing spoon. With the restoration of Charles II in 1660, new regalia were speedily designed and made at a cost of almost £13,000 (over one million pounds in today's money).

St Edward's Crown – carried before the sovereign in the coronation procession by the Lord High Steward – is the 'official' crown of England, and the one used by the Archbishop of Canterbury to crown the king or queen regnant during the ceremony. It was made for Charles II by Sir Robert Viner, who based his design as closely as possible on the pattern of that supposedly worn by Edward the Confessor. Weighing around 5lb, the circlet is embellished all around with gemstones surrounded by diamonds, while above this stand alternate fleurs-de-lys and crosses pattées from which spring two complete golden arches edged with pearls. These arches are important, signifying the wearer as ruler. Without arches, the crown would simply be a coronet. Underneath this is the purple velvet Cap of Maintenance edged with miniver fur.

The Imperial State Crown, perhaps more magnificent than the St Edward's, was made in 1838 for the coronation of Queen Victoria and its spectacular jewels (see page 29) tell a fascinating historical tale. The Black Prince's ruby

Opposite:
The Imperial State Crown, made in 1838 for the coronation of Queen Victoria, is worn by the sovereign at the end of the ceremony and for the procession through the streets. It is also worn at other state occasions such as the opening of Parliament.

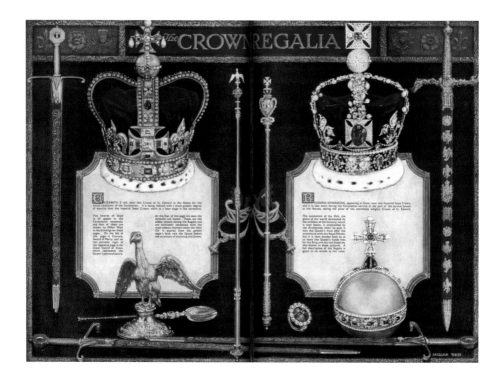

Illustrations of the crown regalia, painted by Millar Watt in *The Sphere* in 1953, show the St Edward's Crown and the Imperial State Crown, four swords of state, the orb and sceptres, and the ampulla and spoon used for the anointing. Next to the orb is the 'Wedding Ring of England', comprising a sapphire cross over rubies and representing the monarch's commitment to her realm and its subjects.

was given to him by Pedro the Cruel after the battle of Nagera in 1367 and was worn by Henry V at Agincourt. The pearls adorning the crown are believed to have once been earrings belonging to Elizabeth I and the magnificent Star of Africa is the second largest stone cut from the famous Cullinan diamond and mounted in 1909. It also includes two huge sapphires – the Stuart sapphire from the crown of Charles II bequeathed by Cardinal York, last of the Stuart line, to George III, and Edward the Confessor's sapphire – as well as four rubies, eleven emeralds, sixteen more sapphires, 277 pearls and over 2,700 individual diamonds. This is the crown traditionally worn by the monarch at the conclusion of the ceremony and afterwards, for the procession back through the streets and, in the case of Elizabeth II, for her famous post-coronation photographs by Cecil Beaton.

In contrast, the Imperial Crown of India, created for George V specially for the Delhi Durbar of 1912, was worn just once. Since it was considered inadvisable to take the crown jewels halfway across the world, a new piece was specially made. George V wore the crown along with full coronation robes in the searing Delhi heat; it was something of an ordeal for the king who wrote in his diary, 'Rather tired after wearing the Crown for 3½ hours, it hurt my head, as it is pretty heavy …' The crown made for Queen Mary for the coronation could rival it in splendour, not least because it boasted the Koh-i-Noor diamond, a gift from the exiled Maharajah Duleep Singh to Queen Victoria in 1850, as well as two more stones from the Cullinan. The Koh-i-Noor, meaning Mountain of Light, was later reset into Queen Elizabeth's crown for the 1937 coronation, the first to be entirely mounted in platinum. She wore this again for her daughter's coronation in 1953 with the arches removed. Traditionally, the Koh-i-Noor is worn only by a queen or queen consort, as there is a long-held belief that it brings bad luck to any male wearer. Interestingly, for earlier coronations, many of the diamonds and pearls worn in a consort's coronation crown were customarily hired from jewellers. If the crown were to go on display, the borrowed gems would be replaced by paste substitutes, crystals and semi-precious stones.

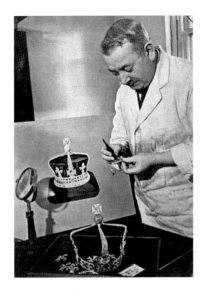

Mr Charles Stone, of Messrs Garrard & Son, the court jewellers, assembling the various parts of the circlet first made for Queen Victoria and modified for each succeeding coronation. The crown was designed with four cross pattées and four fleurs-de-lys with the famous Koh-i-Noor diamond set in the front cross pattée. The crown was adapted for Queen Elizabeth, consort of George VI and later the Queen Mother, by including four complete arches instead of the eight half-arches forming Queen Mary's crown.

The biggest stone from the Cullinan diamond – the 92-carat Cullinan 1, which is the largest flawless cut diamond in the world – is set into the sovereign's sceptre, also known as the Sceptre with the Cross. As the most important of the five sceptres used during the coronation, it is symbolic of temporal power. Such was the belief in this instrument as the embodiment of majesty that even as late as the reign of Queen Anne, the royal assent to all acts of Parliament was given by the monarch touching the sceptre to the parchment on which the Act was written. The Sceptre with the Dove held in the sovereign's left hand, is the symbol of spiritual power. Two more sceptres, the Queen's Sceptre and the Queen's Sceptre with the Dove, are held by a queen consort during the ceremony, echoing those of the king, and the final sceptre, St Edward's Staff, 4 feet 7 inches long, mimics a walking staff – a golden metaphor intended to guide the monarch along life's pathways.

The magnificent Imperial Crown of India, created by Garrard & Son especially for George V to wear to the Delhi Durbar in 1912. The crown contains 6,170 diamonds and a spectacular 34-carat emerald.

27

Queen Alexandra, pictured in her coronation robes by the artist Samuel Begg for *The Illustrated London News*, was the last consort to wear hired jewels in her crown, for the 1902 coronation. Afterwards, the crown was reset with paste stones before it went on display to the public.

The Orb of England (carried by the sovereign – there is a smaller version, originally made for Mary II, held since by queen consorts) is made of two unmarked gold hemispheres (though its appearance is satisfyingly solid), weighs 1.32kg and is covered in more than six hundred precious stones. Its spherical shape, surmounted by a jewelled cross, represents Christ's domination over the world.

The crown, the orb and the sceptre are the popular symbols of monarchy, the three things that a schoolchild might include when drawing the queen. But there are other objects that play a significant role in the coronation ceremony. There are, for instance, the eight extremely heavy maces, descended from the club-like weapons used by soldiers in the Middle Ages, representing royal authority and carried by serjeants-at-arms. There are the Golden Spurs: emblems of knighthood, which are brought to the king or queen by the Lord Great Chamberlain and simply touched on the sovereign's heels before being returned to the altar. The armills (bracelets), a gift from the Commonwealth representing wisdom and sincerity, were reintroduced to the coronation ceremony in 1953, the first time since the reign of Edward VI. Also worn by the queen that day was the so-called 'Wedding Ring of England', symbolising her commitment to her realm and its subjects. The ring boasts a superb sapphire crossed over with rubies and encircled with diamonds to reflect the cross of St George.

Of the five swords of state, the Jewelled Sword of State plays a key role in the ceremony. As its name suggests, it is lavishly encrusted with diamonds, emeralds and rubies, crafted at the bequest of George IV whose fondness for ceremonial bling led to him spending £6,000 on its creation. During the ceremony, the sovereign is girded with this sword before – in a symbolic gesture – handing it over to the Archbishop of Canterbury to show that the power of the state is placed at the service of God.

Along with the anointing spoon, the ampulla is another survivor of the Parliamentarian purge though in comparison to the spoon, it is believed to be of more recent, possibly early Stuart origin. Of pure gold, it is in the shape of an eagle with its wings outstretched and holds the holy oil used to anoint the king or queen.

The Jewel House at the tower safeguards all these dazzling pieces and more, including fifteen silver trumpets with gold-embroidered silk banners, used by heralds at coronations and proclamations. The coronation regalia itself is transported from the Tower of London to Westminster Abbey on the eve of the ceremony under the supervision of the Keeper of the Jewels with an escort of Household Cavalry. It is received at the abbey by the Dean of Westminster and rests overnight in the Jerusalem Chamber, until the following morning when the officiating clergy carry the jewels in procession through the cloisters and into the abbey.

Reverential treatment and secure measures have not always kept the nation's treasures safe from harm. King John was said to have lost the crown

St. Edward's Sapphire; and the Large Pearls, "once the Ear-rings of Queen Elizabeth." (The State Crown.)

The "Star of Africa" (the Largest Cullinan Diamond) in the King's Royal Sceptre; and, above it, the Great Amethyst Orb.

The Drop-shaped Cullinan Diamond (Third Lesser Portion) as Fitted above Queen Mary's Crown.

The Stuart Sapphire in its setting at the back of the State Crown.

The Black Prince's Ruby; and (below it) the Second Lesser Portion of the Cullinan Diamond. (The State Crown.)

The Coronation Ring of William IV., Edward VII., George V., and George VI.

The Koh-i-Noor Diamond; and (below it) the Fourth Lesser Cullinan Diamond, as Fitted in Queen Mary's Crown.

Pages from commemorative issues of magazines allowed readers to get up close to the crown jewels. This page, from *The Sketch* in 1937, displays some of the famous and priceless jewels forming the coronation regalia of George VI. St Edward's Sapphire (top left) in the imperial State Crown is said to have been in the coronation ring of Edward the Confessor, the Star of Africa (top centre) is part of the Cullinan Diamond, found in 1905 in the Premier Mine in Pretoria – the largest piece of which is in the royal sceptre. The Black Prince's ruby (top right) in the imperial State Crown belonged to the king of Granada in the fourteenth century, and the Stuart sapphire (centre bottom) probably belonged to Charles II.

LOSS OF
CROWN JEWELS IN THE WASH

jewels while attempting to cross the Wash, near King's Lynn in 1216. In 1303, the regalia, along with many other jewels and items of gold plate, was kept in the seemingly impenetrable crypt of the Chapter House at Westminster Abbey. But when news reached Edward I that the treasures had been plundered, it was clear

On 14 October 1216, King John, while on a campaign against rebel barons, arrived at the south side of the Wash. As his army crossed the sands, the tide rose unexpectedly and the king's baggage, including, according to legend, the crown jewels, was lost. It was the final disaster in a fairly disastrous reign and the king died of dysentery a week later.

ST. GEORGE'S SPURS
AND THE BRACELETS

"Queen Victoria Crowned and Wearing the Imperial Mantle."
From a water-colour from the Life; by Sir William John Newton. Reproduced by permission of the Trustees of
the British Museum.

THE SWORD OF STATE

CURTANA, OR, SWORD OF MERCY

Symbolic emblems of the coronation ceremony, including (top) the bracelets and spurs used during investiture. Pictured in the centre is Queen Victoria wearing the mantle of cloth of gold.

that only the monks of the abbey could be responsible and all forty-eight of them, including Abbot Wenlock, found themselves languishing for two years in the Tower of London for their crime. In 1671, an Irish soldier, Colonel Blood, described by the diarist John Evelyn as having 'a false countenance, but very well spoken, and dangerously insinuating', made the one and only serious attempt to steal the crown jewels. Having befriended the seventy-seven-year-old Assistant Keeper of Jewels, Talbot Edwards, he arranged to view the jewels with some acquaintances

The notorious Colonel Thomas Blood, looking like a true pantomime villain on a cigarette card from 1911. His audacious attempt to steal the crown jewels in 1671 was foiled; surprisingly, King Charles II pardoned him for the crime.

early one morning. Edwards was bound and knocked on the head with a mallet, while Blood and his accomplices made off with the Imperial State Crown and the orb (the latter stuffed rather disrespectfully into one man's breeches). Blood and his gang might well have pulled off perhaps the greatest jewel heist in history but for the unexpected early return of the keeper's son, who raised the alarm. After a dramatic chase on horseback, Blood was caught and arrested at St Katherine's Dock. Quite inexplicably, he was pardoned by Charles II; who was perhaps amused by the adventurer's rakish audacity. But the escapade led the keepers at the Tower to improve security and visitors were no longer allowed to handle the crown jewels.

An engraving from *The Graphic*, 1885, showing the display of regalia behind bars at the Tower of London, with a yeoman warder keeping watch on the sightseers. Security was tightened after Colonel Blood's failed attempt to steal the crown jewels in the seventeenth century, but the jewels were in danger again in 1841, when a fire broke out in a building next to the Jewel House. The key to the case with the crown jewels could not be fetched in time but a quick-thinking policeman wrenched the bars apart with a crowbar and the jewels were safely evacuated.

PAGEANTRY AND RITUAL

THE RITUAL OF THE CORONATION and the wider programme of events on the day itself follow a carefully staged timetable, with each choreographed set piece imbued with symbolic meaning, historic tradition or religious significance.

Up until the reign of James II, the monarch traditionally resided at the Tower of London for several days before the coronation, it 'being the castell royal and chief house of safety', before setting forth in a magnificent cavalcade for Westminster Hall, where the considerable coronation cast would assemble and organise themselves the following morning for the brief journey to the abbey. This progress, from the tower to Westminster, saw medieval and Tudor London *en fête*; Henry IV for instance, whose coronation was recorded for posterity by Froissart, was accompanied by no fewer than six thousand horsemen, and fountains streaming with bountiful supplies of wine were dotted along the richly decorated route. The restoration of Charles II in 1660 saw this historic pageant played out one final time, Pepys declaring to his diary, 'So glorious was the show with gold and silver that we were not able to look at it'.

The tradition was abandoned when Charles's brother James II came to the throne, the king choosing to spend the saved money instead on jewels for his queen, Mary of Modena, a decision that cannot have done much for his popularity. The state procession from Westminster Hall to Westminster Abbey continued, proceeding on foot to the west door along a covered platform or 'passage', railed in on both sides and covered with blue broadcloth 'strewed with nine baskets full of sweet herbs and flowers' by the King's Herbswoman and her party of handmaidens.

The hall also continued to be the setting for the great coronation banquet held after the coronation service had finished. It must have called for an extraordinarily speedy and efficient turnaround to transform the hall from a ceremonial meeting point, to the scene of a lavish feast catering for hundreds, within a matter of hours. Consider the coronation banquet of James II which had no fewer than 175 dishes served to the king's table alone, numbering among

Opposite:
The Recognition, where the sovereign (here George VI) stands before the assembly and is presented by the Archbishop of Canterbury. Cosmo Gordon Lang, Archbishop of Canterbury, defended the anachronistic character of the coronation in 1937 writing, 'It is no mere paradox to say that the very merit and meaning of these coronation rites is precisely that they are, in a sense, "out of date." How could the wonderful stability and continuity of the national history be more impressively shown?'

Public celebrations of a coronation are not a recent phenomenon, as evidenced by this engraving showing the coronation procession of Edward VI in 1547. The cavalcade is shown passing through Cheapside, festooned with decorations and flags, on its way from the Tower of London to Westminster Hall.

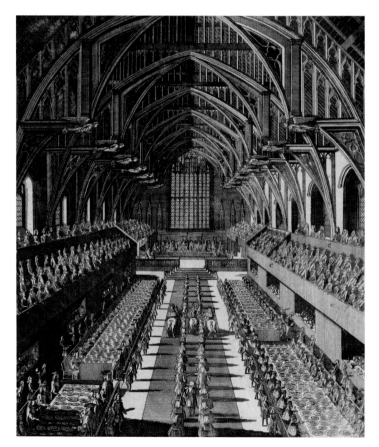

The coronation banquet of James II in 1685. For the spectators lining the gallery, who were not fed, it must have been a mouth-watering but frustrating experience.

them such exoticisms as stag's tongues, 'Udders roasted', 'Twenty-Four Puffins (cold)', 'Trotter Pye', Periwinkles and 'Cavear'. Up to the reign of William IV, the coronation regalia, which are guarded overnight in the abbey's Jerusalem Chamber by Yeomen of the Guard, would be brought to Westminster Hall in the morning to form part of the procession. In more recent times, the abbey clergy, dressed in their ceremonial vestments, would convey the regalia from the chamber, through the cloisters, first to St Edward's Shrine behind the high altar where the anointing oil in the ampulla is consecrated, and then up the nave to the annexe to await and join the assembled procession there.

But before any procession could begin, the congregation had to fill the abbey. In 1953, this involved seating over eight thousand invitees, an exercise in crowd logistics carried out smoothly by the Gold Staff Officers who ushered guests to their seats in the hours leading up to the ceremony. With peers and peeresses, officers of state, heralds, diplomats, overseas royalty, representatives of the armed forces, choristers and clergy all dressed in their finest gowns and ceremonial robes, the effect within the Abbey was remarkable. The artist J. H. F. Bacon was commissioned to paint the coronation of George V for posterity and gave a poetic description of the scene:

> Although I had been there daily for three weeks, it now all had a look of magic. The mighty stone pillars, blackened by time, seemed like the limbs of giants dipping their feet in wave upon wave of picturesque humanity … A pale light descended always from the great windows of the nave which fell and was lost in a mystic gloom. The contrast between this and the shimmer of the silks and the scintillation of the jewels was striking. I recall saying to myself, No painter who ever lived could do this justice. Any attempt at actuality MUST fail; to present even the idea of it, one must perforce fall back on impressionism.

With the abbey filled to the brim, members of the royal family arrived in procession in advance of the sovereign, including, since 1937, the Queen Mother. It was not customary for the dowager queen to attend the coronation, but Queen Mary, a dominating influence when it came to royal ceremonial, was insistent on seeing her son, George VI, crowned. The only queen to see her grandchild ascend to the throne, she unfortunately died only a few weeks before the 1953 coronation. The peal of the ten bells of St Margaret's, Westminster, 'ringing the Queen by', welcomed her arrival and at 11.15 a.m., the 250-strong procession, comprising representatives

Each coronation feast was characterised by the arrival of the King's Champion, described in Debrett's 1902 *Dictionary of the Coronation* as 'the most perfect relic of feudalism'. Since the thirteenth century, the Dymoke family of the manor of Scriveley in Lincolnshire have claimed the right to one of the sovereign's horses, together with saddle, harness, and the gold cup from which the king drank to his champion. In return, the champion would ride into the hall and after a trumpet fanfare, throw down his gauntlet and challenge anyone who denied the king's claim to the throne.

A sketch by Paul Renouard in *The Graphic* of a lady spectator going to take her place among the temporary seating constructed in Westminster Abbey for the coronation of Edward VII. Some seating was accessed via steps and entrances on the exterior walls of the abbey.

Princesses Elizabeth and Margaret Rose in the royal box with their grandmother, Queen Mary, looking straight out onto the coronation theatre where they witnessed their parents' coronation. A drawing for *The Sphere* by J. Finnemore.

from crown, church and state, began to make its stately progress down the rich blue carpet of the nave and choir to the strains of *I was Glad* by Hubert Parry. First composed for the coronation of Edward VII in 1902, the piece incorporated the acclamation by the Queen's Scholars of Westminster School of '*Vivat Regina*' ('Long Live the Queen'), the traditional greeting as the monarch enters the Abbey. The spectacle of the procession in 1953 was described, somewhat emotionally, by the Reverend Doctor Jocelyn Perkins, sacrist of Westminster Abbey, who gave an account of the ceremony in *The Queen* and thought the procession was 'too overwhelmingly beautiful for words … what may be termed poetry in motion. Every single person therein from the Archbishop of Canterbury to the youngest pageboy, walked quietly, reverently and totally devoid of self-consciousness. It was perhaps the most solemn dignified ceremonial ever witnessed by Westminster Abbey.'

With the regalia placed upon the high altar alongside the splendid gold communion plate, and the protagonists positioned in their places in theatre, the coronation rite could begin. The first stage, the Recognition, the most democratic portion of the service, presented the queen to the assembled congregation, which was asked by the archbishop to accept her as 'undoubted Queen of this Realm'. The Recognition is a legacy of the ancient Saxon tradition of ratifying the election of a sovereign by his or her subjects and for

any dissenting voice, it was an opportunity to declare one's opposition though, as far as it is known, such an awkward situation has never arisen. After the abbey's unified voices had affirmed their recognition with a crescendo of, 'God Save Queen Elizabeth', representing the assent of the people, the queen sat on the Seat of Estate to take the coronation oath, a promise to uphold the laws of the land and to maintain the Protestant faith. This stage had formerly taken place towards the end of the ceremony, but a modest shake-up of the ordering of the service in 1953 placed the semi-civil features of the rite together in what seemed a more meaningful arrangement. With the oath and the declaration signed by the queen, she then laid her hand on the Bible and uttered the words, 'The things which I have here before promised I will perform and keep, so help me God.'

Then came the Anointing, the most ancient and holy element of the ceremony. The chrism is poured from the ampulla into the anointing

Elizabeth II in the simple white gown in which she was anointed, with the canopy of cloth-of-gold held over her head by the knights of the garter. There is written evidence in First Recension *ordines* that a similar anointing rite was performed at the coronations of the Anglo-Saxon kings at Kingston-upon-Thames during the tenth century. As the most sacred and intimate part of the ceremony, it was agreed that television cameras would not intrude on the actual moment of anointing.

The Coronation Chair, or King Edward's Chair, in Westminster Abbey, London, shortly before the coronation of George V. It was carved from oak – the four gilded lions at its feet are later additions. Over the years, it has suffered various forms of damage, from graffiti carved by Westminster School boys to an attempt at vandalism during a suffragette protest, but it remains a potent symbol of the British monarchy.

spoon by the Dean of Westminster. He passes it to the archbishop who dips two fingers into the partitioned spoon and anoints the sovereign on the arms, hands, breast and head. The anointing oil contains oils of orange, roses, cinnamon, musk and ambergris and usually a batch is made to last several coronations. However, in May 1941 a bomb hit the Deanery, destroying the phial of anointing oil. The pharmacy that had mixed it was no longer in business but the recipe was found and a new batch of oil made. The Anointing is accompanied by the most familiar music of the coronation, *Zadok the Priest and Nathan the Prophet,* composed by Handel in honour of the coronation of George II and performed at every coronation since.

For this stage of the ceremony, the queen was helped out of the crimson robe of state she had arrived in by the Mistress of the Robes, the Duchess of Devonshire, and took off her diadem. For kings, it is traditionally the Lord Great Chamberlain who aids in the several costume changes required throughout the ceremony. Instead of a diadem, the queen's father, George VI, wore the unadorned velvet Cap of Maintenance for the first stage of his coronation. Over her coronation gown the queen put on a simple, white shift and sat upon the Coronation Chair, under a canopy of cloth-of-gold, held aloft by four knights of the garter.

The Coronation Chair, also known as King Edward's Chair , was made for Edward I to hold the sacred Stone of Scone (also known as the Stone of Destiny), captured from the Scots and sent to Westminster in 1296. The relic, a powerful symbol of Scottish nationalism, had been used by the kings of Scotland for their coronations until its removal to England. After years of controversy over its ownership, the Stone has, since 1996, resided in Edinburgh Castle along with the Scottish crown jewels, with the proviso that it be transported to Westminster Abbey when required for future coronations. Every monarch since Edward I has been crowned on King Edward's Chair, with the exception of Mary I whose chair was sent specially from Rome by the Pope.

Following the Anointing (or Sacring) and the blessing from the archbishop, the canopy-bearers moved away and the queen was dressed in the coronation vestments. First went on the *colobium sindonis*, a linen garment similar to a priest's alb, and then, the *supertunica*, a sleeved long tunic of gold,

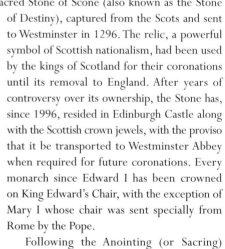

floral brocade with no fastening. These garments, undeniably medieval in style, are based on those worn by Edward the Confessor, whose robes were preserved as relics when Henry III rebuilt the abbey. They were used by subsequent monarchs in the actual rite of the coronation but were then destroyed, along with the crown jewels, following the execution of Charles I.

Clothed in these vestments, the queen remained seated in King Edward's Chair as the next stage, the Investiture, saw each piece of the coronation regalia presented to her. First came the military emblems, the spurs and the swords, then the stole and the imperial mantle went on top of the *supertunica*. The coronation ring was put on her fourth finger, representing the symbolic marriage between sovereign and people, and Lord Woolton presented a glove, provided by the Worshipful Company of Glovers. The orb was held briefly and then handed back so that she could take the Sceptre of

The supreme and pivotal moment of a coronation since the early medieval era; the Archbishop of Canterbury, Geoffrey Francis Fisher, raises St Edward's Crown and places it on the head of Elizabeth II.

the Cross in her right hand and the Sceptre with the Dove in her left and await the supreme moment.

The archbishop ascended the steps to the high altar, took St Edward's Crown in his hands and holding it high for all to see, said a prayer before the crown was brought forward and placed upon the queen's head. Simultaneously, the effect was mirrored as the peers and peeresses placed their coronets on their heads and a crescendo of pealing bells, gunfire and shouts of 'God Save the Queen' marked the historic moment.

Almost three centuries earlier, William III wrote of his own coronation, 'It was a great moment when I actually felt the crown descending upon me and touching my temples, and I could not restrain a thrill, but not of joy ... but of awe, at the responsibilities Almighty God had been pleased to put

A picturesque scene during the coronation of George VI, visualised by Hookway Cowles in *The Sphere*, as the peeresses in the congregation simultaneously put on their coronets at the moment Queen Elizabeth was crowned. Ladies wore tiaras to the coronation and the smooth manoeuvre of placing and securing the coronet behind the tiara required some practice.

upon me'. Queen Victoria felt the same, calling the moment the crown was placed upon her head a 'beautiful, impressive moment'.

After the crowning, the sovereign moved from King Edward's Chair to the throne placed upon a dais in the centre of the theatre. This Enthronement was traditionally the moment when the sovereign enters and takes possession of the kingdom, and when the homage of the nobility, a throwback to feudal society, takes place. At a king's coronation, the queen consort would also sit here after her crowning, slightly lower on the dais than the king, but in 1953 the queen sat enthroned alone and the first person to kneel before her after the archbishop and bishops had done their fealty was her husband, who knelt bare-headed, placed his hands between hers and solemnly said, 'I, Philip, Duke of Edinburgh, do become your liege man of life and limb.'

Wearing the Imperial State Crown and robe of regal purple, Elizabeth II makes her solemn progress down the nave following her 1953 coronation. Her six maids of honour, all daughters of dukes or earls, wore Hartnell-designed dresses and carried the queen's train, with the help of silk handles artfully stitched to its underside.

The last stage of the coronation was the communion service where the queen, after offering bread and wine at the altar, and making a gift of 'an ingot or wedge of gold of a pound in weight', knelt at a faldstool (a folding stool) while the rite proceeded. Finally, she returned to the throne as the *Gloria in Excelsis* was sung and the blessing given.

One more change of clothes was to come before the newly crowned monarch could lead the procession out of the abbey. During a brief retirement to St Edward's chapel, the ceremonial vestments were taken off. An ancient rule stated that because the vestments were relics of the Confessor – or

An unusual view of the shrine of St Edward in Westminster Abbey, by Douglas Macpherson in *The Sphere*, showing its function during the coronation ceremony (here that of George VI). After the king is crowned, he passes through the door on the south side of the high altar into St Edward's chapel. The queen at the same time passes into the chapel via a door on the north side of the altar. The king, standing before the altar, delivers the sceptre with the dove to the archbishop who lays it on the altar. He is then disrobed of his Royal Robe of State and arrayed in a robe of purple velvet and, wearing his Imperial Crown, receives the orb from the archbishop. Their majesties then proceed through the choir towards the west door of the abbey.

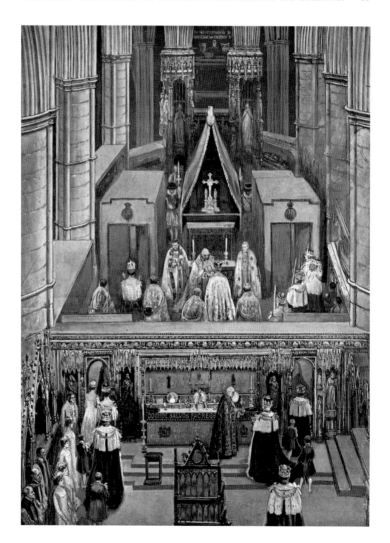

at least reproductions of relics – they were the property of the abbey. In earlier periods, the abbey's clergy did a little recycling and royal mantles – even though they had been created at the king or queen's own expense – were transformed into rather magnificent ecclesiastical copes. The crimson robe the sovereign had arrived in was replaced with a magnificent version of regal purple with a cipher and a border of wheat ears and olive branches embroidered in silk woven at Lullingstone Castle, and the Imperial State Crown was substituted for King Edward's Crown. Carrying the sceptre and orb the newly crowned Elizabeth made her way to the west door where the golden coach waited.

The return journey, a distance of around five miles, wound its way triumphantly along Whitehall, Pall Mall, St James's Street and Piccadilly, into Hyde Park through the Marble Arch onto Oxford Street, Regent Street, Haymarket and the Mall. The procession itself, with 29,200 participants marching ten abreast on foot and six abreast on horseback, stretched two miles, necessitating the regiments at the front to start off from Birdcage Walk the minute the service was concluded. The solemnity of the coronation ceremony gave way to festive pageantry and celebration as the procession rumbled along the famous streets. Despite the cold and rain, hundreds of

King George VI and his consort, Queen Elizabeth, enthroned and in full regalia as portrayed by Fortunino Matania in *The Sphere*. The king holds the Sovereign's Sceptre and Orb, and the queen holds the smaller Queen's Sceptre and the Queen's Sceptre with Dove. The embroidery on the queen's sumptuous train was in the shape of the floral emblems of the Empire and was stitched at the Royal School of Needlework.

The coronation procession of Queen Victoria from 28 June 1838, illustrated in the 'Correct Representations on the Occasion of Her Majesty's Coronation'. Consisting of two vast panels, each 25 feet long, it is a detailed record of the participants, from the Life Guards at the front, to the carriages of the Duchesses of Kent and Gloucester and the Queen's State Coach, pulled by eight horses and accompanied by Yeomen of the Guard.

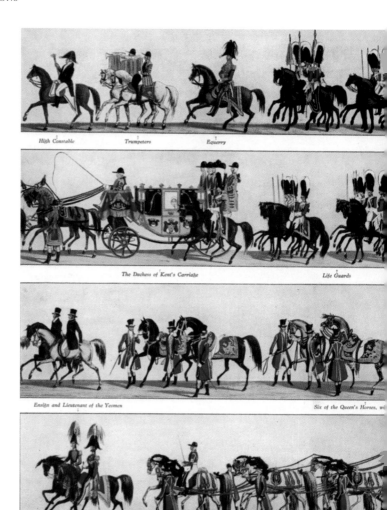

thousands of spectators cheered and waved their newly crowned queen at every stage of the route and later, those who had gathered outside Buckingham Palace were rewarded by the queen appearing on the balcony, a coronation tradition first introduced by her great-grandfather, Edward VII. When darkness fell, the queen appeared once more to turn on the 'lights of London'. As the palace was floodlit, a cascade of lights illuminated the Mall and Trafalgar Square all the way to the Tower of London. It was a fitting climax to a remarkable day and the general consensus was that this modern staging of an ancient ritual had been an outstanding success.

Life Guards

The Duchess of Gloucester's Carriage

The Queen's State Coach The Knight Marshal Capt.-General of the Royal Archers Marshalmen

Below:
The King's Greys pulling the State Coach, carrying King George VI and Queen Elizabeth from their coronation at Westminster Abbey on 12 May 1937. The coach was built for George III, who drove in it to open Parliament in 1762, and has been used for every coronation since that of George IV. Illustration by A. C. Michael in *The Sketch*.

MISHAPS AND
MISMANAGEMENT

O N 24 June 1902, two days before the coronation of Edward VII was due to take place, five thousand children from the East End of London were entertained at a special coronation fete in Victoria Park. The event included a Punch and Judy show and comedy cricket match played by several notable members of the music-hall profession. In the midst of the fete came the news that the king was ill. The *Illustrated London News* wrote in its 5 July issue, 'Without the slightest warning the light-hearted babble of our Coronation show was silenced by a menace which for days held the nation in acute suspense.' This menace was appendicitis, a condition with a high mortality rate in 1902. The king, overweight and not in the greatest of health, had complained of stomach pains during the morning of 24 June but refused to allow any illness to delay his crowning, an event for which he had waited a not insignificant time, and which had already been postponed until the conclusion of the Boer War. But it became clear that immediate medical treatment was required, and when a bulletin was posted outside Buckingham Palace at 11.15 a.m. stating that a surgical operation was necessary, the nation held its breath. A number of Indian officers who were being conducted around Fulham Palace, on hearing the news from the Bishop of London, immediately went to pray for the king in the field opposite the palace; around the country, other impromptu intercessions for the king's recovery took place.

On the day originally set for the coronation, those who had tickets for Westminster Abbey instead attended a service for the king at St Paul's Cathedral while sightseers, according to the *ILN*, 'moved listlessly about the route of the procession, taking note of the neglected decorations and imagining regretfully what the day might have been. Here and there, seat-holders, probably from the country, actually occupied their places, and sat watching the traffic.' Happily, the procedure was a success and, after a period of convalescence upon the royal yacht, a fitter and considerably trimmer King Edward VII was crowned on 9 August 1902. But many of the events that had been planned around 26 June went ahead anyway. Schoolchildren who had been invited to view the procession from Marlborough House

Opposite:
King Edward VII resplendent in his coronation robes and glowing with health, as pictured by E. A. Cook in *Boy's Own* magazine. When the king's postponed coronation finally took place on 9 August 1902, the king, often known as 'Tum-Tum' due to his generous girth, looked considerably trimmer.

Newspaper boys – the bearers of bad news. The preparations for the coronation of King Edward VII were almost complete when the king fell ill with appendicitis.

An impressive living display formed by the crew of HMS *Terrible* in honour of the coronation of King Edward VII in 1902. It was organised by Captain Percy Scott RN for display on 26 June. Unfortunately, due to the king's illness delaying the coronation, the feat was rather overlooked but Captain Scott must have gained some satisfaction when this illustration was published in *The Graphic*.

were entertained instead by the prince and princess of Wales with a luncheon, and other coronation fetes for children around London took place including one in Battersea Park attended by Princess Louise, who was treated to the picturesque sight of 20,000 marching children. The Coronation Naval Review at Spithead, comprising some 120 vessels, was already assembled; Queen Alexandra acted as proxy for her husband at a review of Indian troops; and in Whitehaven the country's largest coronation bonfire, standing at more than 120 feet, was lit anyway. Perhaps most disappointed may have been Captain Percy Scott, who arranged for 220 of his crew on HMS *Terrible* to climb down the ship's side and form the words, 'God Save the King' on the day of the coronation.

The actual event was not without its hitches. Frederick Temple, Archbishop of Canterbury was over eighty years old, somewhat infirm and myopic. Throughout the ceremony, his doddery state was a concern to the king who kept whispering, 'I am very anxious about the Archbishop.' At the moment of crowning, Temple put the crown on back to front and his attempts to rectify the mistake made matters worse. Later, as the archbishop struggled to get back on his feet after paying homage, the king kindly offered him his hand. George VI found himself similarly having to take the lead during

A bonfire prepared in Norwich for the coronation of King George V in 1911. Similar bonfires were constructed for the previous coronation but when it was postponed, they were lit anyway and built again for the re-scheduled coronation six weeks later.

The Duchess of Leeds and the Countess of Annesley watching hopefully for their cars following the coronation of George VI on 12 May 1937, while other peeresses turn their backs in resignation. A torrential downpour meant that a large proportion of the 7,500 guests at Westminster Abbey – most in full ceremonial robes – was left stranded for hours.

his 1937 coronation, noting in his diary the attempts by the dean to put the *colobium sindonis* on him inside out and the supporting bishops struggling to find their place when it came to the oath, only to find that when the archbishop tried to help, he 'held his book down for them to read, but horror of horrors his thumb covered the words of the oath.' The Lord Great Chamberlain was trembling so much the king had to vest himself, and one of the bishops clumsily

stepped on his train. After the ceremony, a sudden torrential downpour led to a quite spectacular muddle in the elaborate arrangements for getting the abbey guests away. As the general public, seeking cover, blocked the roads, chauffeurs found it increasingly difficult to find their passengers. The result was the incongruous sight of hundreds of stranded peers and peeresses still in

their robes and coronets, with muddied dress hems and ermine, having had no food since the early morning, and with no discernible way of getting home. Five hours after the ceremony was over, *The Sphere* reported there was still a solid mass of guests 100 yards long at one entrance alone. It was an undignified and soggy conclusion to the day.

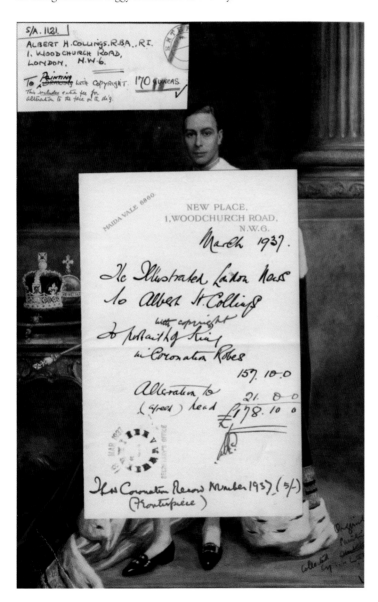

Opposite and left: A portrait of Edward VIII by Albert Collings for the Coronation Record of the *Illustrated London News* had to be hastily adjusted when the king abdicated in December 1936. The invoice stuck over the new version indicates that Collings was paid 21 guineas to change the head of Edward VIII for that of his younger brother, George VI.

The events five months earlier had of course changed George VI's destiny. By the time the abdication of his elder brother was certain, the plans and preparations for his coronation, scheduled for 12 May, were well underway and rather than halt the organisational juggernaut, the smoothest solution seemed to be to maintain the original date and carry on regardless, albeit with a new king. Fortunately, the Duke of York (as he then was) had attended a number of the committee meetings in the king's place and was already reluctantly half-prepared for what was to come. The crisis had far-reaching effects, many of them commercial. At the offices of the *Illustrated London News*, preparation of their special Coronation Record Number was all but complete. Pages of photographs documenting Edward VIII's life were interspersed with specially commissioned paintings of the king in his coronation robes. No doubt anxious to avoid the costs incurred by starting afresh, the artists Fortunino Matania and Albert Collings were simply paid an additional fee to alter the heads on their portraits. Magically, for the sum of 21 guineas on top of the 159 guineas 10s. already paid to Collings, King Edward VIII transformed into King George VI and the paper kept more or less to its budget.

The 1831 coronation of William IV came at a time of acute economic depression and the king saw little point in staging an extravaganza, especially when the cry of 'Reform' was in the air. He was eventually persuaded to take part in what became known as the 'Penny Coronation', or 'Half Crownation', with George I's old crown padded out to fit him and ushers in the abbey obliged to pay for their own costumes. The result was a coronation that cost just £43,159, a sixth of the cost of his elder brother's a decade earlier. Although such frugality was a cause of mirth among satirists, William IV's tight grip on the purse strings also gained him popular approval. Gossips and press alike, however, were scandalised at the absence of the Duchess of Kent, whose excuse was ostensibly that the length of the day would be taxing on her daughter, Princess Victoria, though the fact that Victoria was placed behind the king's brothers in precedence in the procession was regarded as closer to the truth. *The Observer* newspaper was openly critical of the duchess's actions and *The Times* indignantly wrote that she had 'Refused to attend, yes, refused to attend'! There was no love lost between the bluff, old king and the mother of the heir-presumptive, but it did mean that Princess Victoria was not given the opportunity of observing the rituals of the service she herself would endure within seven years.

At her own coronation, in June 1838, the Dean of Westminster was sorely missed, as he was too ill to attend. As it was, the queen was given the orb at the wrong moment, the Bishop of Exeter fell over and the Archbishop of Canterbury pushed the coronation ring onto her finger with such force, she had to stifle a cry and soak her hand in cold water afterwards in order to remove it. When she was ushered through to St Edward's Chapel,

Queen Victoria looking the picture of regal serenity after her coronation in June 1838, despite enduring a somewhat muddled ceremony.

she was horrified to see the altar in the sacred shrine covered with sandwiches and wine bottles. Less affected, Lord Melbourne partook of a glass of wine.

George IV's coronation was characterised not only by its eye-watering extravagance, but also by his refusal to allow his estranged wife, Caroline of Brunswick, to attend. Determined to take her rightful place, Caroline endeavoured to gain entry to the abbey. The doormen, hired prize-fighters, stuck doggedly to their instructions of 'No ticket, no admission' regardless of who it might be, and Caroline, 'a good deal agitated,' was eventually forced to admit defeat, travelling away from the abbey in her carriage to cries of, 'For shame, for shame' from the largely sympathetic crowd. Two weeks later, she was dead. Aside from this interruption, the ceremony seems to have been uncomfortable for all concerned. It was a particularly hot day and the two thousand candles in the abbey added to the overpowering heat and caused several ladies to faint, while the peers and peeresses found their finery ruined by the 'profuse globules of melted wax which were continually falling upon them'. The king himself, corpulent and trussed into an outlandish costume of silver and gold, with a train modelled on that of Napoleon and so long it needed eight train-bearers, spent much of the ceremony mopping his perspiring brow, rallying occasionally to leer at his mistress Lady Conyngham. Little wonder he declared afterwards, 'I would not endure again the sufferings of that day for another kingdom!'

The coronation in 1761 of his father, George III, seemed beleaguered by forgetfulness. There were no chairs for the king and queen to sit on, nor a canopy for them to walk under. The Sword of State was forgotten and so the Lord Mayor's was hurriedly borrowed as a substitute. The king appeared more knowledgeable of the ceremonial than the heralds, who made 'numerous mistakes and stupidities', and as James Henning concluded 'The whole was confusion, irregularity and disorder.' By the time the bungling ceremony was over, the king and queen had to drive back to Westminster Hall in darkness. It can have been of little comfort to the king when Lord Howard of Effingham, acting as Earl Marshal admitted, 'It is true, sir, there has been some neglect, but I have taken care that the *next* coronation shall be regulated in the exactest manner possible.'

George I's coronation in 1714 was a trial for both him and the officiating clergy for he knew no English and they no German. Instead, the ceremony

WILLS'S CIGARETTES.

QUEEN CAROLINE REFUSED
ADMITTANCE TO THE ABBEY.

Queen Caroline (Caroline of Brunswick) was refused entry to Westminster Abbey during the coronation of her husband, George IV, who had given express instructions that she was not to be admitted. It was a final insult from her estranged husband; she died a fortnight later.

was conducted in faltering Latin. Language barriers had had a more devastating effect at the coronation of William I. At the moment of acclamation, the roar of approval from the assembled Anglo-Saxons was heard outside by Norman soldiers and mistaken for an English revolt. Panic and confusion ensued and the Norman guards charged the crowd and set fire to surrounding buildings, a ghastly episode in the history of coronations.

The tendency to see certain events and choices during a coronation as prescient of a sovereign's future proved remarkably pertinent in the case of Charles I. As for his father, James I, the original date of his coronation was postponed due to plague. The king was clothed in white rather than the traditional purple, which some viewed as an omen of his future misfortunes; other occurrences, such as the discovery that the wing on the Sceptre with the Dove was broken, and the earth tremor felt in the abbey during the ceremony all added up to a collective sense of foreboding.

Those prone to superstition saw similar omens in the coronation of Charles I's son, James II. According to contemporary accounts, at the very moment the archbishop placed St Edward's Crown on the king's head, the Royal Standard floating from the White Tower was ripped asunder. The crown itself refused to sit obediently on James's head (though one wonders if this might not have had something to do with the king's voluminous wig), leading his queen consort, Mary of Modena, to remark that, 'there was a presage that struck us, and every one who observed it.' Hokum mixed with the benefit of hindsight these coronation hiccups may have been, but they helped feed the myths of both unfortunate monarchs.

Elizabeth II may have endured fluctuations in her personal life but in more than one thousand years of history, few reigns have been more peaceful or prosperous; and her coronation was near-faultless perfection. 'The Queen did her part with great recollectedness and simplicity, and without any outward trace of nervousness,' wrote the Dean of Westminster, Dr Alan Don. This was undoubtedly in part due to a full fortnight of rehearsals, four of which were attended by the queen. The result was a coronation free of stumbles and forgotten lines, life-threatening illness, missing regalia, maligned consorts and thankfully, massacres. It was, concluded the Duke of Edinburgh afterwards in typically off-hand fashion, 'Not a bad show.'

Cigarette card depicting the ill-fated Charles I at his 1626 coronation. The king's choice of white for his costume was reckoned to be an omen of his future misfortunes.

CORONATION FEVER

SINCE THE CORONATIONS of the medieval age and their extravagant processions through London from the Tower to Westminster, ceremony and ritual were increasingly underpinned by mass celebration and public participation – a phenomenon that had developed into a global event by the twentieth century. In 1953, it seemed that anyone who wished to could experience the coronation.

The day selected for Elizabeth II's coronation was predicted by meteorologists to be fine and sunny. But with a typical British unpredictability, London woke that morning to dark clouds and drizzle. However, for the two-million-strong crowds lining the 5½-mile processional route, thirty thousand of whom had slept overnight on the pavement, the unseasonal weather did little to dampen spirits.

Perhaps a number of them had taken some of the advice doled out by women's magazines in numerous 'How to survive the coronation'-style articles. *Good Housekeeping* made what might be considered a rather excessive suggestion: 'Your most important member that day will be your feet. Wear the most comfortable pair of shoes you possess, and if you suffer from a twinging corn, pay a visit to the chiropodist a few days beforehand ...' It also outlined a highly prescriptive packed lunch to take along, its wholesomeness designed to maintain energy levels during the gruelling wait (malt or crisp breads with a nourishing filling, 'to provide you with your proteins and vegetables for that day'). Other recommended items for spectators included a flask of hot tea, wrapped boiled sweets and most appropriately in the event – a rain hat. Hundreds bought periscopes, in reality the only way to glimpse the magnificent procession except for the hardy street campers who had staked a claim at the front. Seventy-three-year-old widow Mrs Zoe Neame from Speen in Buckinghamshire began her coronation day at 8 a.m. on 30 May when she took her place in Trafalgar Square at the foot of the Charles I statue, wearing nothing more than a cardigan over her silk frock and with a supply of egg sandwiches and fruit her only sustenance. Having sat out for every royal occasion since 1921, Mrs Neame

Opposite:
A picture taken of the surging crowds at the South Africa House side of Trafalgar Square shortly after daylight on the morning of the coronation of George VI. Soon afterwards, barriers had to be closed to all but ticket holders. Even then several thousands gathered outside, particularly in the Strand where the road rises slightly, consoling themselves with a long-distance view through periscopes and by listening to the mighty volume of cheering.

'Ho, Billy, this IS rippin'! – a reg'lar Royal box'. In this cartoon published in *The Graphic*, two little street urchins find a brilliant vantage point to Edward VII's coronation – through the legs of a policeman's horse.

Among the decorations inspired by the coronation of George VI and Queen Elizabeth were these life-size effigies of the royal couple, the focal point of the elaborate decorations on the facade of the London Pavilion.

admitted to a reporter from the *Daily Sketch*, 'I do it for the thrill of it. I never catch cold. I've never been ill, at least, not seriously.' If she had been, then St John's Ambulance had stocked up on forty thousand high-energy glucose sweets to dispense to fatigued and fainting spectators.

A few had been lucky enough to secure tickets for one of the grandstand seats erected along the route. Among these was a young Margaret Thatcher, who recalled, 'The tickets were an even wiser investment than Denis knew when he bought them.' Lady Violet Bonham Carter, who was in her seat in a stand on the Mall by 7 a.m., described the miserable sight of some in the crowd, 'wrapped in soaking newspapers and plastic mackintoshes but burning with loyalty & full of good humour, tho' many

had been there all night.' Spirits needed to be high – many of the campers on the Mall had had to endure a further influx of day-trippers who flooded into London during coronation week to see the graceful arches spanning the Mall, and the flags, flora and decorations adorning the rest of the capital.

Coronation-themed souvenirs and decorations – which were to embellish many homes and streets around the country – were produced in their millions, though official souvenirs had to be approved by the Coronation Souvenirs Committee of the Council of Industrial Design. Aside from the inevitable flags, bunting and mock shields bearing the Union flag or royal standard ('very Woolworths' as one rather snobbish Mass Observation interviewee concluded of the street decorations in her area), coronation fever touched everything from hair pins to silk scarves, commemorative cups and plates to paper lanterns. *Good Housekeeping* listed numerous commemorative items including a wicker basket in the shape of a crown, designed to hold Sun-Pat peanuts; also available were bath salts, a crown-shaped cake tin, and sun-suits for boys and girls in specially designed coronation fabric, while biscuit tins were produced in their millions. Coronation mugs were given free to every schoolchild while the queen herself personally selected a special cup, produced by Spode-Copeland, to be presented to the children of workers from the Royal Estates.

Women's magazines were awash with suggested outfits for 'this coronation year'. *Everybody's Magazine* featured a range of what seem impossibly glamorous evening dresses from couturiers such as Victor Stiebel and Lachasse

A silk handkerchief commemorating the coronation of Edward VIII. Thousands of commemorative items had already been produced before his abdication and despite efforts by the government to curb the sale of products featuring him, they still proved popular souvenirs with the public.

Coronation fever seemed to touch every conceivable product in 1953. Here, regal hairpins feature small crowns, and a picture of a youthful Princess Elizabeth on the packaging.

Women at the Royal Doulton potteries at Burslem, pictured decorating and glazing the coronation beakers to commemorate the coronation of George V in 1911 and given to 100,000 children at the Crystal Palace fete on 30 June that year.

A nostalgic advertisement from 1953 for Spangles sweets, which draws on the excitement surrounding the coronation as inspiration.

while *The Tatler* suggested a dress of printed rayon taffeta from Marshall & Snelgrove for 'the woman with a narrow budget'. For those untroubled by such concerns, an Asprey advertisement displayed a tiara for anyone needing one at the last minute! Burberry, rather appropriately, advertised its famous raincoats in special coronation issues and lingerie manufacturer Berlei even produced a special 'Coronation Corselette' to mould the figure into 1950s perfection underneath a new dress.

For the vast majority of the British population, the coronation was experienced via the medium of wireless and television. It was the year that television took off, with many people investing in one for the first time in order to watch the coronation and an estimated twenty million people nationwide viewing at least half an hour of the ceremony. Neighbours were invited to huddle round available sets, sharing in the experience of seeing what was, because of the poor picture, an 'ermine-draped ectoplasm floating about a rather bizarre séance', with the steady commentary by Richard Dimbleby generally agreed as a broadcasting triumph.

In order to keep going throughout this televisual marathon, *The Daily Sketch* suggested snacks and drinks including a 'Coronation Cooler'

A creative challenge for the ambitious 1950s cook, this advertisement for Chivers jellies features a quite spectacular crown-shaped dessert – a fitting centrepiece for any street party.

comprising Moselle sparkling wine, soda water and strawberries. Fried sandwiches filled with cheese and 'Ideal sauce' were the suggestion of TV cook Jacqueline Rose. *Good Housekeeping* devised far more elaborate menus, drawing inspiration from Francatelli, maitre d' to Queen Victoria, for one menu. A new recipe for 'Coronation Chicken', the now classic combination of chicken, apricots and curried mayonnaise created by Constance Spry, was distributed widely via magazines, and we can only hope that a number of adventurous housewives attempted the recipe from Chivers jellies – a superbly ostentatious jelly crown decorated with cream, cherries and angelica.

For many Britons, street parties were the focal point of their coronation celebrations. Across the country, neighbourhoods collected contributions and enjoyed donations from local businesses in order to give children the party of a lifetime. In halls and streets bedecked with flags and bunting, lavish teas included such delights as blancmanges, ice cream, fruit and sweets (this in a country only just emerging from the privations of rationing). Fancy dress, dances, conjurors and Punch and Judy shows added to the fun, particularly in working-class areas that had embraced the coronation festivities with fervour.

A familiar sight up and down the country in June 1953 were children's street parties in celebration of the coronation. This party, in an unidentified but bunting-adorned location, is typical, with children enjoying teatime treats, and parents and babies in prams lining up behind the tables for the photograph.

FURTHER READING

Roy Strong, *Coronation – From the 8th to the 20th Century*
    (Harper Perennial, 2006)
Various, *The Coronation Book of Queen Elizabeth II* (Bounty Press, 2006)
James Wilkinson, *The Queen's Coronation – The Inside Story*
    (Scala Publishers, 2011)
Jeremy Paxman, *On Royalty* (Viking, 2006)

PLACES TO VISIT

Westminster Abbey, London SW1P 3PA.
    Website: www.westminster-abbey.org
    Described as a 'must-see living pageant of British history'.

Reims Cathedral, Place du Cardinal Luçon, 51100 Reims, France.
    Website www.reims-cathedral.culture.fr
    Location for the crowning of French kings and the inspiration
    for Westminster Abbey's layout.

INDEX